GH00732044

Hoyle on Poker explained

Poker
According to Hoyle

with additional ramblings by
Palamedes

ꝑ

Parsimony Press
1999

ACKNOWLEDGEMENTS

Grateful thanks to Steve Shaiman, Peter Pathe and
Dean Ballard, who as mathematicians claim to know
all about poker, and who therefore made several picky
corrections. These have probably ruined the book,
but at least we will sell three copies.

Cards by courtesy of Thai Airways International

First published in Great Britain in 1999
Second impression 2000
Parsimony Press Limited
West Huntspill, Somerset

A CIP catalogue record for this book is available from
the British Library

ISBN 1 902979 01 X

Editor: Robert Norton
Typesetting: Olivia Norton, Barbara Wragge & Eiichi Kono
Printed by: Tien Wah Press, Singapore

Contents

Palamedes, a Grecian chief, son of Nauplius, king of Euboea, was sent by the Greek princes to oblige Ulysses to join the expedition to Troy. Ulysses, reluctant to leave his wife Penelope, feigned madness, but Palamedes exposed the deceit. Ulysses in consequence conceived a bitter enmity against him, and forged a letter supposed to be written by King Priam to Palamedes treating of the delivery of the Greek army into Trojan hands. He also had a large sum of money concealed in Palamedes' tent, and by these means caused him to be convicted of treason and stoned to death.

Palamedes is credited with much learning and ingenuity, the addition of certain letters to the alphabet of Cadmus, and the invention of various games and devices.

Oxford Companion to English Literature

How the book works:-

Hoyle is in italics. The rest is Palamedes, or what other sources he quotes.

History of Poker

According to that best of all Encyclopedias, the 11th edition Britannica, the origin of poker has been ascribed by most writers to *Il Frusso*, an Italian game of the 15th century. From this came the game of Primiera, called in Spain *Primero*, and *La Prime* in France, where it was elaborated into *L'Ambigu* or *Le Mesle*.

In England, the game was played under the name of *Post and Pair*, of which the modern *Brag* is only a variation. But Mr R F Foster proved that, though poker is probably a descendant of *Primero* and perhaps of a much more ancient Persian game called *As ras*, it is not a development of the English *Brag*, but was introduced from France into the colony of Louisiana, the name being merely a mispronunciation of *Poque*, a game described as early as 1718 in the *Academie universelle des jeux*. It is still played in Germany under the name *Pochen*. The earliest mention of the game in America is in G. B. Zieber's *Exposure of the Arts and Miseries of Gambling* (1843), and it is probable that poker was generally played on the Mississippi steam-boats as early as 1830, twenty cards being used, "full-deck poker" with 52 cards being invented later. "Draw-poker" was introduced about 1860. Jack-Pots were introduced about 1870.

Principles of Poker

There are many advantages to being dead.
One of the best is that instead of being restricted
to what was known when you are alive you can
get to know all the things that have been
learned since you died.

Poker is one of those. Poker is the king of card
games (bridge may be the queen) and is the
least vulnerable to bad luck, and as such is the
closest to backgammon. Like backgammon,
poker is about counting and odds. The more
care you take the more often will you win. The
more you ignore numbers the more likely you
are to lose to someone who has taken more
trouble than you.

There is another aspect to poker which is a
source of great entertainment to us up here.
It is what we call the Martini Principle. The
Martini Principle affects men much more
rigorously than it does women, particularly in
activities like driving, and watching games like
football, baseball and cricket. Under the
Martini Principle – for nobody admits to
making a less than perfect dry martini – few
men admit to driving motorcars badly,
knowing nothing about football, or playing
poker badly.

More wage packets have disappeared on night shifts into the pockets of people who have made the best of the martini principle than have been spent on paying the electricity bill. Before you start learning more about poker at least make it your aim to learn enough to stop too much leakage to vanity. It is no fun losing money, and it is no fun playing poker unless money is at risk.

Perhaps it is for this reason that Hoyle started his instruction by talking about betting. But I haven't asked him, since up here we tend to regard talking about money as a bit vulgar and childish.

> *Any number from two to seven can play. The game uses fifty-two cards, which rank: A K Q J 10 9 8 7 6 5 4 3 2. Anyone can deal the first hand.*

> *A betting limit is agreed upon and then each player purchases from the banker a certain number of chips. The one on the left of the dealer, called the "age", puts up one of these chips for a "blind" on every deal, except in jack pots.*

We can go into jackpots later. I find it hard to accept the many other variations that people have made, mostly because they tend to give less skilful players more of a chance than they deserve. When the element of luck is increased it equally favours both the skilled and the unskilled, and gives less reward to those who have studied to improve.

> *Five cards are dealt to each player, one at a time. The player to the left of the age can "straddle" before he looks at his cards by putting up double the amount of the blind. If he straddles, the player on his left may straddle him again by doubling the last amount put up, and so on; but if any player in his turn refuses to straddle, the player on his left cannot do so.*

This procedure is again something of an unnecessary gamble. It is somewhat out of fashion in the late 20th century, although I am told it will revive again towards the middle of the 21st. Few poker players at this time even know what is meant by 'age', 'blind' and 'straddle'. Nevertheless it is quite appropriate that Hoyle should have begun with the betting procedure, since winning at poker depends entirely on betting the right amount at the right time. What is at stake is visible on the table. The chances of your hand being the best are also capable of calculation. The chances of your hand being the winning hand are by no means always the same, since a better hand than yours may not remain in the game.

A popular variation, for example, is that a

player must win two, or even three, hands to claim the pot. In this instance the player who has already won a hand is likely to bet more heavily than those who have not, simply because in one case the winnings are certain and in the other they are not. Prudent players are disinclined to add substantially to the winnings of their opponents, once their chances of winning are less than they were before.

If you don't remember what is meant by Straddle or you are not sure who or what is the Age, go back and read the beginning again, since you won't understand what follows if you don't know the vocabulary.

> *The object of the game is to get certain combinations of cards. A player may improve the hand originally dealt to him by drawing to it, first throwing out any cards that do not make up a poker combination, hoping to draw in their place some cards that will match those already in his hand. When a hand cannot be improved by drawing to it, it is called a "pat" hand.*

If there is truly a pat hand, it will tend to be a straight or a flush or a full house. The value of these hands is high, as you will see. Other players, if they believe that there is truly a pat hand, will know not to bet against it with a hand that is less strong. But because there is

the chance that the person who professes to
need no cards is bluffing, and hoping to collect
all the stakes without being challenged, there is
certainly a reason for risking some additional
stake if you hold a hand that is capable of
improvement at good odds.

Hand Values

In the following table, the first hand given is the best and the others follow in their order:

Royal flush
The five highest cards in the same suit.

Straight flush
Sequence and suit, but not the five highest cards.

Four of a kind

Full hand
Three of any kind, and a pair of another kind. (This is now known as a Full House)

9

Flush
All one suit, but not all in sequence.

Straight
Any sequence of five cards, not in one suit.

Three of a kind
with two cards which are not a pair.

Two pairs
with a card which does not match either pair.

A pair
with any three cards which are of no value.

Highest card
The highest card in the hand decides. Cards below it decide ties.

In straights, the ace may rank below the deuce or above the king. In deciding between two hands of the same class, the higher rank wins; three tens beating three nines. If the hands are both two pairs, the higher pair wins. (If, as may happen, the two pairs are the same, then the highest odd card wins.) Jacks and deuces will beat tens and nines. In two flushes, the rank of the cards wins – the order being Spades, Hearts, Diamonds, Clubs. In a straight flush, the actual head of the sequence wins: 7 6 5 4 3 will beat 5 4 3 2 A.

In addition to the standard hands, it is sometimes agreed, especially in the Southern States of America, to play five extra hands. These are (in ascending order)*:*

A blaze, or 5 court cards
Beats two pairs; but loses to three of kind.
(Notice that it must be at least two pairs if it is to contain five court cards.)

A tiger, or little dog
7 high, deuce low; without pair, or flush.
Beats a straight; loses to a flush.

Big dog
*ace high and 9 low, any card of the sequence
being missing. Beats a straight or little dog;
loses to a flush.*

A skip, or Dutch straight
*a sequence of alternate cards of various
suits. Beats two pairs and a blaze.*

15

Round-the-corner

*any straight in which the ace connects the
king with the deuce. Beats three of a kind;
but the lowest straight will beat it.*

*The rank of these hands is entirely wrong,
being apparently fixed by guesswork. A skip
should come between a flush and a straight.
A tiger, big or little dog, between a flush and
full. A round-the-corner between a full and
a blaze. A blaze between a round-the-corner
and four of a kind.*

As I said, get into this kind of variation only
when you are playing for stakes of no value. Or,
of course, when you are among better players,
whose skill advantage you want to diminish.
It is also wise to decide beforehand whether
you play real odds, or Southern U.S. odds.

How to Play

You now know the value, and you have an idea of how to bet, and of the importance of making sensible assessments. So we can begin.

> *After the cards are dealt, the players look at their hands and declare to play or to pass. Each in turn to the left of the age, or of the last straddler if there has been any, puts into the pool, if he plays, double the amount of the blind, or of the straddle. This is the "ante" and if any player in his turn wishes to increase it, he may do so to any amount within the betting limit. When the ante is raised, each player to the left must see the raise or pass out, losing what-ever they have already put into the pool. Should another raise the ante still higher, all must see the last raise, or pass out.*

There have already been two rounds of betting. The first, the blind, before anybody saw their cards, and the second, the ante, when people have seen their cards but have not yet tried to improve their hand by changing some of the cards. You will see that there is an opportunity here for people who are winning, or people who are richer than other players, to apply pressure on those with less money to drop out before they lose too much. If you are in this position it is best to stop playing than to leak what little you have into a sequence of hands in which you are unable to play because you cannot match the level of betting. Even if you come up with a royal straight flush you wouldn't be able to use it unless somebody was prepared to lend you the money you would need to show it. A betting limit agreed in the beginning helps restrain the power of the rich. But the consequences of playing out of the level you can afford are generally that you will lose, however skilful you are, and should therefore be avoided.

In the 20th century, people have tended to skip the whole betting sequence and content themselves with an ante, and then betting in the following sequence.

> *When all those who are going to play have anted an equal amount, the dealer gives cards to each in turn, beginning on his left, helping each player to the full number asked for before helping the next man. Every player must discard before he draws.*

> *When all have been helped, the player to the left of the age makes the first bet or passes out. If the age has been raised out before the draw, the player on his left must still make the first bet, as the privilege of the age never passes, even to a straddler.*

When a bet is made, each player in turn must do one of three things:
  - call, by betting an equal amount;
  - raise, by betting more;
  - or pass out, throwing up his hand.

Any player who has been raised may raise again when it comes round to his turn, and these raises may continue indefinitely, provided no player raises the amount of any previous bet by more than the betting limit. When no one will raise the last bet made, all those who have called show their hands for the pool.

If any player puts up an amount that no one will call, either before or after the draw, he takes the pool without showing his hand. If a call is made, all those in the pool must show their hands to the board, and the best poker hand wins.

No one who either calls or is called is allowed to say "that's good" to another hand, and throw up his cards without showing them, and any player at the table can demand to see his hand.

This is important. The only way anybody can avoid showing their hand is by dropping out before the betting is finished, or by betting enough to have everybody else drop out rather than match the bet. Bluffing is a useful tool in poker, but it stops being so if it is over-used. There is much to be learned by remarking on the hands of other players and comparing them with the betting procedure that each player followed – who raised, and who matched the bet, for example.

Let us go to the 11th edition of Britannica for a summary. They say that

'The game is played by from 2 to 6 or even 7 people with a pack of 52 cards. The player who wins the cut for deal shuffles the pack, which is then cut by the player at his right. He then deals five cards, one by one, to each player. If a card is faced during the deal the player must accept it; if two are exposed a new deal must ensue. Before the deal is complete the player at the dealer's left, who is said to hold the age, and is called "the age", places (or puts up) on the table in front of him half the stake for which he wishes to play. This is called blind. The player at the age's left then looks at his hand and announces whether he will play. If his hand seems too weak, he throws his cards away face-down, and "drops out" of the game.

'If he elects to play, he puts up his ante, which is twice the amount of the blind. The other players, including the dealer, then either come in, i.e. elect to play, each putting up his ante, or, deeming their hands worthless, drop out.

'The age, who has the last say, may then himself drop out, forfeiting his half-stake already put up, or he may come in and make good his ante, i.e. put up his unpaid half of the blind.

'Each player in his turn has the privilege of increasing the stake to any amount not exceeding the limit, which is always agreed upon before the game begins. Thus, if the limit is £1, and the age has put up 2p as his blind, any player may, when his turn comes to declare whether he will play, say, "I play and make it 50p (or as much as £1) more to draw cards," at the same time placing the ante (4p) plus 50p (or £1) in the middle of the table.

'Thereupon all the other players, each in turn, must see the raise, i.e. pay in the additional sum, or drop out of the game, forfeiting what they have already paid into the pool. The "age" being the last to complete, is in the best position to raise, as a player who has already completed is less likely to sacrifice his stake and withdraw from the game. On the other hand each player has the right, in his turn, after paying the extra stake called for, of raising it further on his own account, and this goes on until the players who have not dropped out have paid an equal sum into the pool and no-one cares to raise further.

'Each player then throws away as many of his five cards as he chooses, and receives from the dealer new ones in their place. In this supplementary deal no player may accept a faced card, but receives one in its place after all the other players have been served. The number of new cards taken by each one should be carefully noted by the other players, as it gives a valuable clue to the probable value of his hand.'

By the end of the 20th century, I regret to say that it has been far too common to find that people stop bidding when it gets back to the dealer instead of going on to the age. This plainly makes the art of bidding less elegant, and I think should be discouraged. The eleventh edition continues

'Each player having received new cards called for, the betting is opened by the player sitting at the age's left, should he consider his hand worth it; otherwise he throws down his cards (face down) and is out of the game, and the next player (whom we will call C) makes the first bet, which may be of any amount up to the limit, but is usually a small one, with a view to later developments.

'The next player, D, either

- drops out,

- trails, i.e. puts up the amount bet by C
(also called seeing and calling), or

- raises C's bet: in other words puts in the
amount bet by C plus as much more (within
the limit) as he cares to risk.

'This raise on D's part means either that he
thinks he holds a better hand than C, or that he
is trying to frighten C out. The last manoeuvre
illustrates the principle of the bluff, the most
salient characteristic of the game of poker. If C,
with two small pairs in the hand, bets 12p, and
D, with a hand of no value whatever, covers, or
sees C's bet and raises it to a pound, it is very
likely that C will throw down his cards rather
than risk a pound on his own by no means
strong hand. In this case C has been bluffed by
D, who, without even having to show his cards,
wins the pool, although intrinsically his hand
was far inferior to C's. The ability to bluff
successfully depends upon self-command, keen
observation, judgment and knowledge of
character, so as to attempt the bluff, when the
bluffer is sure that there are no very strong
hands out against him. Otherwise he will surely
be called in his turn, and, having nothing of
value, will lose the pool, besides suffering the
ignomiy of throwing away his money for
nothing.

'Two players with strong hands will often raise

each others bets repeatedly, until one of them calls the other, upon which the hands are shown and the stronger wins. The complete hands of the caller and the called must be shown. The common practice of throwing away unshown, for purposes of concealment, a losing hand that has called is illegal. No player who is not called is obliged to show his hand, so that the company is often in doubt whether or not the winner has bluffed. When two hands are of exactly equal value the pool is divided.

'The game is often varied by a player going blind, i.e. raising the ante before the deal. Another variation is straddling the blind. This is done by the player sitting next to the age, who puts up twice the amount of the blind with the words "I straddle". This has the effect of doubling the stake, as every player must then pay twice the amount of the straddle (instead of the blind) in order to play. The straddle does not carry with it the privilege of betting last, but merely raises the amount of the stake.'

You will see that if the player to the age's left straddles, he is only putting up the same amount as he would have put up anyway. The advantage is that he may frighten off some players who might interfere with his plans. The disadvantage is that he is committing himself to adding the other half when the betting reaches him again if he is not to drop out.

Poker Laws and Penalties

The pack must be offered to the player on the dealer's right to be cut, or it is a misdeal. If a player deals out of turn, he must be stopped before the last card is dealt or the deal stands.

A misdeal does not lose the deal. It is a misdeal if a card is found faced in the pack in dealing before the draw; or if the dealer gives six cards to more than one player; or deals a wrong number of hands; or exposes more than one card.

Any card faced in the act of dealing before the draw must be accepted by the player to whom it falls; but two cards so exposed constitute a misdeal.

Any hand of more or less than five cards, any part of which is lifted or looked at, is foul.

If one player has less than five, the other hands being correct, the dealer must give him another card from the top of the pack the moment his attention is called to it. If one player has more than five, the other hands being correct, he can ask the dealer to draw a card, or he can demand a new deal, provided no one has anted.

If one player has six cards and the player next to him has four, neither having lifted nor looked at any card, the dealer may draw from the surplus hand and give the card to the short hand. If one hand has been lifted or looked at, while the other has not, the dealer shall make the adjustment as before, but then the hand looked at is foul. The other may be played. Any card or cards once discarded or thrown into the deadwood, cannot be taken back under any circumstances. Any counters once placed in the pool, except under a mistake as to their value, whether in the player's right turn or otherwise, cannot be withdrawn.

No player but the dealer need reply to any question as to how many cards he drew, and the dealer is not allowed to give any information as to the draw of any player but himself. If the dealer is asked how many he drew, he must reply correctly, if the player asking is still in the pool but has not made a bet.

Any card found faced in the pack when dealing for the draw must be thrown into the deadwood.

Any card exposed by the dealer when dealing for the draw must be placed among the discards, and the player must wait until

all the others, including the dealer, have
been helped before the card is replaced.

If any player asks for a wrong number of
cards, he may correct himself if he has not
lifted or looked at any of those laid off,
provided the next player has not been
helped. If the next player has been helped,
the one in error must discard so as to take
all the cards asked for. If he has already
discarded too many, his hand is dead.

If the dealer gives a player a number of
cards not asked for, his attention must be
called to it before any of the cards laid off
are lifted or looked at, and the dealer must
correct his mistake. If others have been
helped in the interval, they keep their cards.
If a player allows another on his left to be
helped out of turn, he must play his hand
pat or pass out. If he has already discarded,
his hand is dead.

Any player who borrows to raise must
afterward borrow to call. There is no
penalty for miscalling a hand in the
showdown, as all five cards in the hand
must be shown to the table. If a foul hand
is shown, it takes the pool unless some
player has a fair hand to dispute it. If two
foul hands are shown, the pool remains
until the next deal.

You should take the trouble to learn these, (which seem to imply a dealer who appears to be dealing with his feet) if only to avoid having a game spoiled by argument. Each one of these will probably occur sooner or later and it is as well to know what should be done.

Calculating odds

There are two ways you can equip yourself
to consider the odds. Real professionals have
practically all the permutations in their heads.
But if we are to assume that you don't want
to play for a living in Las Vegas it should do
to show you how to use the brains that you
were given.

Let us take the flush problem as a start. You
are playing with four other people, and you
have been dealt four hearts. Among five players
you know that a flush is a winning hand, being
beaten only by a full house, fours, or more.

Right.

25 cards have been dealt, and 27 remain
unseen. There are 9 hearts among the 47 that
are not in your hand. You have a little worse
than a one in five chance of getting another
heart. Not one in four.

Nevertheless of the ones not in your hand there
are 20 you will not be able to get at and 27 still
available for dealing. You can assume that the
odds therefore are still that of the 9 hearts, any
one of which you want, four will be among the
other players and five will be in the pile from
which cards can be drawn. Here therefore the

odds would be 5 out of 27, slightly worse than
9 out of 47. But still five to one, roughly speak-
ing. This is only a probability. The odds are
really still 9 out of 47, the same, wherever the
cards lie. For that matter, all nine may be
together with the first one on top for you to
draw. But the odds are very much against it.

At this point you have other considerations.
How much is already on the table, and how
much will it cost you to draw. It also affects
your actions according to how near you are to
the dealer and what other people have done.

If there has been some straddling, and there is
already some money on the table before it is
your turn to bet or pass you have to assume
that somebody has got a reasonable hand.
Matching the stake is probably a good bet at
five to one. If you fail to get the other heart,
and you can expect that you will fail, you can
drop out.

The best you can get if you fail will be a pair.
Although a pair of aces is usually enough to
win among five people. If there has been some
moderately heavy betting and most people are
still in you can expect that the winning hand
will be at least three of a kind. Better then to
throw in.

If there has not been much betting you have

a good chance of winning on a pair of aces or kings. But in principle I think it is foolhardy, even though your keeping four and asking for one card may also be interpreted by the other players as your having two pairs and drawing for a full house. Were that the case, they will tell you, your chances of finding a matching card would be 4 out of 47, or about one in twelve, and unless you are a consummate actor and can show exactly the right amount of concealed delight, anybody with three of a kind will bet against you.

This example, apart from showing you how to calculate, should also show you that you must guard against trying to salvage a win with inferior cards when you have been disappointed in your draw.

While we are on the subject, let us look at two pairs. The chances of your filling to make a full house are about one in twelve. But if you keep the higher pair your chances of making three or four of a kind are three out of twenty-three and a half, there being two others of that pair floating around. This is more like one in eight and is a better bet, even though the hand is not so formidable as a full house.

You should be warned, however, that you have just the same chance of getting a third card of the pair you discarded. Don't sulk. Don't claim you are unlucky. Don't, above all, start to feel sorry for yourself. You were right to keep the higher pair, and you should have known that you stood an equal chance of matching the wrong pair.

Remember that in broad terms you should only expect to win one hand in five. The trick is to win more in that hand than you lost in the other four. Improve your play, and you can expect to win one hand in four, or even three, not because your luck has changed but because you are more likely to improve your hand in the draw than are your opponents.

There are some hands, however, where only the dullest player will do the proper thing. If you get a sequence of four in a suit you will have two ends to get a straight flush to. You will be drawing one. The down side is that you may fail but still get a flush. Moreover there is nothing else you can go for. The sensible alternative is to chuck it in, especially if there is very little of your money on the table. But go for it. People will assume you have two pairs, and if you get it you are likely to win well, since people will think they are betting against two pairs if you don't raise by too much, and have them believe you got a full house. If you didn't get it, who cares? Such a hand is too rare to pass up.

If the gap is in the middle you can only

reasonably hope for a flush, which is more than twice as likely as filling the straight. Here you are back to the slightly worse than one in five chance of filling it. It is a question of what you can win off the table against what you are paying to stay in. Better than six times your potential total stake and it is worth trying.

Odds table 1

No jokers

	Possible	Probability	Odds (1 in)
Any hand	2598960	1	1
Royal flush	4	0.53908	649740
Straight flush	36	1.38517	72193
4 of a kind	624	0.00024	4165
Full house	3744	0.00144	694
Flush	5108	0.00197	509
Straight	10200	0.00392	255
3 of a kind	54912	0.02113	47
2 pair	123552	0.04754	21
1 pair	1098240	0.42257	2
High card (any other)	1302540	0.50118	2

Two wild jokers

	Possible	Probability	Odds (1 in)
Any hand	312510	1	1
Royal flush	4	1.26	790628
Straight flush	36	1.13834	87848
5 of a kind (illegal)	78	2.4664	40545
Flush	5108	0.00162	619
4 of a kind	360	0.00296	338
Full house	46800	0.0148	68
Straight	77760	0.02459	41
3 of a kind	293280	0.09274	11
2 pair	737100	0.23307	4
1 pair	1171456	0.37042	3
High card (any other)	821528	0.25977	4

Odds table 2

Having in hand	To make the hand below	Chance is
1 pair	To get 2 pairs (3 card drawer)	1 in 4
1 pair	To get 3 of a kind (3 card draw)	1 in 9
1 pair	To improve either way average value	1 in 3
1 pair and 1 odd card	To improve either way by drawing 2 cards	1 in 7
2 pairs	To get a full hand drawing 1 card	1 in 12
3's	To get a full hand drawing 2 cards	1in 16
3's	To get 4 of a kind drawing 2 cards	1in 24
3's	To improve either way drawing 2 cards	1in 9
3's and 1 odd card	To get a full hand by drawing 1 card	1 in 15
3's and 1 odd card	To improve either way by drawing 1 card	1 in 12
4 straight	To fill when open at one end only or in a middle as 3,4,6,7 or A,2,3,4	1 in 12
4 straight	To fill when open at both ends as 3,4,5,6,	1 in 6
4 flush	To fill the flush drawing 1 card	1 in 5
4 straight flush	To fill the straight flush drawing 1 card	1 in 24
3 card flush	To make a flush drawing 2 cards	1 in 24

How the others behave

Apart from the business of calculating odds, on which too much can never be said, you should also consider the deductions you can make from the behaviour of other players.

For example, somebody who draws four cards is probably somebody who is becoming disheartened, and is keeping an ace or a king in the hope of making a high pair or better. With each card they have about a one in twelve chance of getting a pair or better, so among four cards they have about a one in three chance of getting a pair to their card, or better. The actual odds are complicated by the fact that they may get a different pair, or improve their hand in some other way. They may, after all, get three more in which case they deserve to take the money you lost because you calculated the proper odds and lost.

Somebody who draws three cards has either got a pair or wants you to believe they have. They are probably looking at one in eight chances to improve their hand. Again, slightly better than that to improve in other ways, but not to an extent that it will materially affect your calculations.

The person who draws two cards is probably

trying for a fourth to three of a kind, and is
unlikely to get it. But it can also be a bad and
optimistic player keeping a pair of fours and an
ace. In due course, after a few hands, you will
find out which is the more likely. Nevertheless
you should approach betting against a probable
three with caution. If you pay attention, you
can learn a great deal about the other players
from the hands you lose.

The person who draws one card is most
probably holding two pairs. But there are other
possibilities. They could be hoping for a flush.
They could be trying to fill the ends of a straight.
They could even be trying to put a card in the
middle of a straight. Their chances of succeeding
are no better than yours would be, and it is
likely that they will drop out before risking any
more chips. But it is plainly worth while watching closely as they look at what they have been
given. You will learn nearly as much as you
can deduce from their betting if they stay in the
hand instead of dropping out.

The person who draws none is either sitting
on a straight or a flush or better, or is bluffing.
If they elected to bluff they would certainly put
some pressure in betting before the draw,
before the other players knew they were going
to draw none. But so would they if they had
a good hand. Even a straight, the lowest hand
that nobody would draw to, will beat three of

a kind, so the best course is to let the poor
fellow get away with as little as possible, then
it doesn't matter if it was a bluff. If this comes
up too often you can assume that there is
enough of a likelihood of it being a bluff to at
least encourage somebody to see the hand.

It is difficult to teach anybody anything about
tactics since there can be bluff and double bluff,
and even triple bluff. But triple bluff to one
person is only bluff to another player.

People who play often together learn each
other's habits. People who are playing with
strangers may plan to create a persona that
towards the end of a session will come in to
harvest the chips. For example, if somebody
bluffs twice, and is seen twice, and does not
appear to have lost much, you may find that
later on they will give the impression that they
are bluffing, will suck everybody in and then
show the hand that they have been waiting for
all evening. Had they not bluffed before, they
might have found nobody to put up serious
chips against their winning hand. For one of
the sadnesses is that when one player has a very
good hand it is unlikely that any of the others
have one in the same league. Spectacular wins,
when there are two or more players with good
hands betting against each other, happen
rarely, and mostly in the movies. Winning is
mostly squeezing wins out of moderate cards,

a little at a time. Every once in a while your
two pairs will lose to a three. Or your three to
a full house.

Yet in the long term you don't want to win
a lot. The game should be fun for all, both
winners and losers. Those who crow over their
big wins, and grumble over their losses will find
after a while that there a fewer people who
want to play with them.

Those who have played poker a lot will have
noticed that when you have been winning and
you are inclined to let a hand go to a player
who has lost too much it isn't at all easy. It is
when you try to fill a straight in this instance
that the card comes up.

I sometimes wonder if there is somebody up
here who is interfering in the laws of chance.

Variations on Play

Jack Pots

This is an addition to draw poker which is now invariably played. When no one will ante to draw cards, the deal passes to the left, but the next hand must be a jack pot. Each player puts up an amount previously agreed upon, and no player can open the pot for the purpose of drawing cards or betting upon his hand, unless he holds a pair of jacks, or a hand that will beat jacks. Anyone holding this opening qualification, in turn to the left of the dealer, can "open" for any amount within the betting limit. After it is once "opened" any other players can come in and draw to anything or nothing, as in the ordinary game, provided they will put up the amount for which the pot is opened. The opener of a jack pot must always place his discard under the chips in the pool, but no other player is allowed to put his discard there.

Jack pots are sometimes played when there are only two persons that will ante, one being the age. Both antes are withdrawn without playing the hands, and the next pot is a jack. Another way is to make the first deal of all a jack, and to put a "buck" in the pot with the chips. The winner of that pool takes the buck with it, and when it comes round to his deal it is another jack, the buck being put up again to go to the winner of that pool, and so on. It is sometimes agreed that when hands of unusual strength are shown in a call, such as a full, or fours, that the next deal shall be a jack, or even a round of jacks. Sometimes the game is nothing but jack pots, each dealer in turn putting up for the whole table.

If no one can open a jack pot, each player puts up one white chip and the deal passes, this being continued until some one will open. A player is not obliged to open, even when he has openers; but if he passes, he cannot come in and open it if all the others pass.

In jack pots, the opener always makes the first bet. If he will not bet, the choice falls to the player on his left, and betting proceeds normally.

If the opener is raised out before the draw, by some player making it cost more to draw cards than the opener cares to pay, he must show his entire hand to the table. But after the opener has drawn cards, if he is still in the pool but will not bet, or will not see a raise, he need show openers only, because it is no one's business what he got in the draw.

If the opener has a pair, and also four cards of a flush or straight, he can split the pair to draw for the stronger hand. His discard being always placed under the chips in the pool will be there to show what he had, and at the same time he is not obliged to betray his game by announcing that he is splitting, because he always puts his discard in the pool, whether he splits or not.

If the opener has not the necessary qualifications, he forfeits whatever he has put into the pool if he discovers the error before he draws. Those who have come in on the false opening go on and play for the pool just as if it had been legitimately opened. If the false opener does not discover his mistake until he has drawn cards, he must put up for all the other players in the next jack.

A later variation with considerable support requires the opening hand to be raised in the next deal if there are no openers in the first deal. Thus the second deal needs a pair of Queens to open, and the third a pair of Kings.

The disadvantage of this is that it tends to discourage play. Somebody who opens with two aces is off to a good start. Nobody with less after the draw is likely to stay in.

Jack Pot Laws

Any player who has once passed cannot correct himself and open if any player on his left has passed in the interval.

If a player opens without the proper qualification, his hand is dead and all he has put in the pool is forfeited. If any player has come in against the false openers, the pot must be played for.

If a false opener draws cards, he must ante for the whole table for the next jack pot as penalty; but if he plays his hand pat, the others drawing cards, he is not liable to this penalty.

The eleventh edition summary might also be helpful.

'The regular game is often varied by occasional Jack-pots, which are played once in so many deals, or when all have refused to play, or when the player deals who holds the buck, a marker placed in the pool with every jack-pot. In a jack-pot each player puts up an equal stake and receives a hand.

'The pot must then be opened by a player holding a hand of the value of a pair of knaves (jacks) or better. If no player holds so valuable a hand the deal passes and each player adds a small sum to the pot or pool. When the pot is opened the opener does so by putting up any sum he chooses, within the limit, and his companions must pay in the same amount or "drop".

'They also possess the right to raise the opener. The new cards called for are then dealt and the opener starts the betting, the play proceeding as in the regular game. If Progressive Jack-pots are played, the minimum value of the opening hand is raised one degree every deal in which the pot is not opened.

'Thus the opening hand must in the first deal be at least a pair of knaves; but if the pot is not opened the minimum for the second deal is a pair of queens, for the third pair of kings, &c.'

The Britannica entry is anonymous but the use of the word 'regular' twice in the explanation of jack pots could not have been by an English-man. Since it is clearly by an American I have maintained that Hoyle had a hand in it. In reply he merely says anonymous is anonymous. Thus, I am unable to tell whether he is being modest about his contribution, or hoping that I will give him credit for a far more lucid and economical explanation than in the original book.

Deuces Wild

This may be played with the ordinary pack of 52 cards, or with the joker added, or with the "stripped pack" of 44 cards only, leaving out the threes and fours, and with or without the joker.

Any player holding a deuce may call it anything he pleases, even if he has a duplicate of that card in his hand. The same is true of the joker, if in the pack. The best possible hand is four deuces and the joker. Five of a kind is the next best, then a straight flush, four of a kind, full house, flush, triplets, etc.

In case of ties, the natural cards are better than those represented by the deuces or joker, because it is harder to get the natural cards. Three actual fours will beat a four and two deuces. Before laying down his hand a player should be careful to call its full value. If he goes in on a queen and two deuces and draws a pair of eights, it is a mistake to call the hand a queen full, as it is really four eights.

Stud Poker

This is the same as straight poker, except that the first card to each player is the only one dealt face down, the four others being dealt face up, but only one at a time in each round. Each player takes a look at his own "down card".

When the second card is dealt to each player, the one who has the highest card showing has the privilege of making the first bet. If he will not bet, he may pass until he sees who will. If a bet is made, each player to the left must call, raise, or drop out. Those who previously passed must now call or drop out. Whether any bets are made or not, another card is given to all who are still in the pool, also face up, and the player who has the best hand showing in his two cards has the first say.

As long as two or more are in the pool, the cards are given out until each has five, four of them face up. The final bets are then made, and after a call is reached, the hands are shown. Straights are not played.

Seven card stud

Another 20th century variation is seven card stud.

Two cards are dealt down, the third card is dealt up and people bet as in five card stud, with the highest card starting the betting. The next three cards are also up and treated the same way, the highest hand starting the betting. The last card is down and betting continues normally after that, four cards being visible and three only visible to each player. In North Carolina they have a variation called hi-lo, where the pot is split between the highest and the lowest hand, to give the poorer player more of a chance.

Whiskey Poker

Each player puts an agreed amount in a pool. There is no betting or raising. The dealer gives five cards to each player, one at a time, dealing one to a widow in each round, just before dealing to himself.

The widow remains face down. Each player in turn to the left can take it in exchange for his own hand, which must then be placed on the table face up, or he can pass, or he can knock, to indicate that he is satisfied with the hand dealt him. If he takes the widow, any following player can exchange any one of his cards for any one on the table, or he may exchange his whole hand. Drawing continues until some one knocks.

If no one will take the widow until it comes to the dealer he must take it or turn it up, for each player to draw to.

The moment any player knocks, he means that he has drawn all the cards he wants.

If a player knocks before the widow is taken, it is turned up at once. After a knock, each of the other players has one draw, and the hands are then shown, the best poker hand taking the pool.

Peek Poker

There are two ways to play this game, in some cases seven cards being dealt to each player, in other cases eight, all one at a time. With seven cards, the first two are dealt to the players face down, as in Stud Poker. The remainder are dealt face up. When eight cards are dealt, the last is also face down, five face up.

The players examine all their down cards and then discard and draw, one card at a time in order to the dealer's left. Bets are made after each draw, the best hand showing betting first. No matter what card is discarded, five must be left face up after the draw. When a final call is made, the drawing stops and five cards are picked out of the seven, or eight, to show for the pot.

Table Stakes

This is simply a variation in the betting limit. Instead of limiting each raise to so much, each player is allowed to bet what he has on the table, but no more. Any player who is raised beyond the amount he has in front of him, but who wishes to play his hand, may call for a "sight". If three or more are betting when one calls for a sight, the amount that the sight player would win if he had the best hand is set aside, and the others can go on raising. The player who called for a sight has a show for the first part of the pool only. If he wins it, he takes it, and the others show for the rest of the bets. If he has not the best hand, the whole pool goes to the winner.

No player can add to his stake on the table during the play of a hand, nor can he take down any of his chips.

Freeze Out

This is a variety of table stakes, in which each player starts with an equal amount, and no one is allowed to buy or borrow more. As soon as one player loses his stake, he is frozen out. The others continue, until only one remains, who takes all the money put up.

Poker competitions tend to follow this rule.

Glossary

Age	*The player to the left of the dealer.*
Ante	*The second half of the blind*
Blind	*Half the stake for which the age wishes to play, put up at the opening of play.*
Buck	*The buck is a marker which is put with the chips in a game of jack pots. The winner of the pool will take the buck, which will be played as a jack, when it is his turn to deal.*
Chips	*Counters*
Deadwood	*Discard pile*
Foul hand	*If one player has six cards, and another has four, the dealer may draw a card from the surplus hand, and give it to the short hand. However, if one hand has been lifted or looked at, it is foul, although the other hand may be played.*
Misdeal	*It is a misdeal if a card is found faced before the draw; if the dealer gives six cards to more than one player; deals the wrong number of hands; or exposes more than one card.*

Openers	*A hand on which a jack pot may be opened, ie. a pair of jacks, or a hand that will beat a pair of jacks.*
Pass	*To retire from the hand, or to drop out*
Pat hand	*When a hand of cards cannot be improved by drawing other cards, it is known as a 'pat hand'.*
Pochen	*A version of poker played in Germany*
Pool	*Chips or counters that have been placed in the middle of the table (bets placed)*
Poque	*Early version of poker, introduced originally from France*
Showdown	*Placing the cards face-up on the table after a call*
Sight	*Type of betting used in Table stakes. A player may call for a 'sight' if they have raised beyond the amount in front of them. The amount that the player would win (if he had the best hand) is set aside, while the others can continue to raise. The player who called for a sight can show his cards for the first part of the pool only. If he wins, he may take it, and the others show for the rest of the pool. If he does not win, the entire pool goes to the winner.*

Splitting	*Opening a jackpot with a pair, holding four cards of another suit, then discarding one of the pair, in the hope of making a flush.*
Straddle	*The player on the left of the age may put up twice the amount of the blind, thus doubling the stake*
Stripped pack	*44 cards, leaving out the threes and fours, with or without the joker*
Widow	*The extra hand dealt, such as in Whiskey poker*
Wild cards	*Cards (usually the deuces) which are open in value, and suit.*

Bibliography

Archer Method, (The): An Expert's Guide to Winning at Poker, *John Archer*, (1978)

Basics of Winning Poker, (The), *J. Edward Allen*, (1992)

Body Language of Poker,(The), Mike Caro's Book of Tells *Mike Caro*, (1994)

Caro's Fundamental Secrets of Winning Poker, *Mike Caro*, (1996)

Complete Guide to Poker, (The), *Ros Henry, and Brian Phillips* (1995)

Fundamentals of Poker, (The), *Mason Malmuth*, (1996)

How to Play Winning Poker, *Avery Cardoza*, (1993)

How to Win at Poker, *Belinda Levez*, (1997)

New Poker Games, *Mike Caro*, (1984)

Scarn's Guide to Modern Poker, *John Scarne*, (1984)

Theory of Poker,(The), *David Slansky*, (1994)

Thursday Night Poker: How to Understand, Enjoy-And Win *Peter O.Steiner*, (1996)

Total Poker, *David Spanier*, (1995)

Win at Poker, *Jeff Rubens*, (1984)

Winning Poker for the Serious Player, *Edwin Silberstang*, (1992)

You can look on the internet for more.